# My Feelings

By

Grace Jones

## Crabtree Publishing Company

www.crabtreebooks.com
1-800-387-7650

**Published in Canada**
**Crabtree Publishing**
616 Welland Avenue
St. Catharines, ON
L2M 5V6

**Published in the United States**
**Crabtree Publishing**
PMB 59051
350 Fifth Ave, 59th Floor
New York, NY 10118

Published by Crabtree Publishing Company in 2017

First Published by Book Life in 2016
Copyright © 2017 Book Life

**Author**
Grace Jones

**Editors**
Grace Jones
Janine Deschenes

**Design**
Danielle Jones

**Proofreader**
Crystal Sikkens

**Production coordinator and
prepress technician (interior)**
Margaret Amy Salter

**Prepress technician (covers)**
Ken Wright

**Print coordinator**
Katherine Berti

**Photographs**

Thinkstock: Cover images

All other images from Shutterstock

Printed in Hong Kong/012017/BK20161024

**Library and Archives Canada Cataloguing in Publication**

Jones, Grace, 1990-, author
        My feelings / Grace Jones.

(Our values)
Issued in print and electronic formats.
ISBN 978-0-7787-3246-4 (hardback).--ISBN 978-0-7787-3289-1 (paperback).--
ISBN 978-1-4271-1889-9 (html)

        1. Emotions--Juvenile literature.  I. Title.

BF561.J66 2016          j152.4          C2016-906651-7
                                        C2016-906865-X

**Library of Congress Cataloging-in-Publication Data**

CIP available at Library of Congress

# Contents

Words that look like **this** can be found in the glossary on page 24.

# What are Feelings?

Do you feel happy, sad, angry, scared, shy, or **worried**? These are all feelings.

sad

worried

A person can have many different feelings at the same time.

sad

happy

Your feelings do not stay the same all the time. You may feel happy when you are playing with your friends. You may feel sad if you break your toy.

# Can you tell how each of these children are feeling?

7

# Happy

I laugh when my friend tells me a joke.

When you are happy, you may smile and laugh.

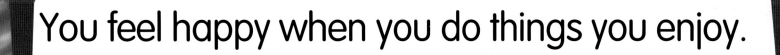

I feel happy when I paint a picture.

You feel happy when you do things you enjoy.

9

Sometimes other people do things that make you feel happy.

10

Other times you might feel happy if you do well at something at school or at home.

# Sad

sad

Many different things can make you sad.

When you are sad,
you may frown or cry.

13

I felt sad when my friend moved away.

Sometimes things happen that make you feel sad.

You might feel sad if you cannot play with your friends.

15

# Angry

You can get angry for many different reasons.

You might be angry with yourself or at someone else.

You might feel angry if you think your mom or dad are not being **fair**.

Other times you might feel angry if someone hurts or **annoys** you.

# Scared

scared

You feel scared when you are **frightened** by someone or something.

You might be scared of sleeping in the dark.

You might try and hide from someone or something that scares you.

If you feel scared, remember you can talk to your mom, dad, or an adult you trust.

**Talking about your feelings with someone can make you feel better.**

23

# Glossary

**annoy** To bug or bother someone

**fair** Treating all people the same way

**frightened** To feel afraid or worried

**worried** To feel uncertain or concerned

# Index